SUPER SIMPLE
FARM
CRITTER CRAFTS

Fun and Easy Animal Crafts

Alex Kuskowski

Consulting Editor, Diane Craig, M.A./Reading Specialist

Super Sandcastle

An Imprint of Abdo Publishing
abdopublishing.com

abdopublishing.com

Published by Abdo Publishing, a division of ABDO, PO Box 398166, Minneapolis, Minnesota 55439. Copyright © 2017 by Abdo Consulting Group, Inc. International copyrights reserved in all countries. No part of this book may be reproduced in any form without written permission from the publisher. Super SandCastle™ is a trademark and logo of Abdo Publishing.

Printed in the United States of America, North Mankato, Minnesota
062016
092016

 THIS BOOK CONTAINS RECYCLED MATERIALS

Editor: Liz Salzmann
Content Developer: Nancy Tuminelly
Craft Production: Frankie Tuminelly
Cover and Interior Design and Production: Colleen Dolphin, Mighty Media, Inc.
Photo Credits: Mighty Media, Inc.; Shutterstock
The following manufacturers/names appearing in this book are trademarks:
Elmer's® Glue-All®, Sharpie®

Library of Congress Cataloging-in-Publication Data
Names: Kuskowski, Alex, author.
Title: Super simple farm critter crafts : fun and easy animal crafts / by
   Alex Kuskowski ; consulting editor, Diane Craig, M.A./Reading Specialist.
Description: Minneapolis, Minnesota : ABDO Publishing, [2017] | Series: Super
   simple critter crafts
Identifiers: LCCN 2016000309 (print) | LCCN 2016001347 (ebook) | ISBN
   9781680781618 (print) | ISBN 9781680776041 (ebook)
Subjects: LCSH: Handicraft--Juvenile literature. | Domestic animals--Juvenile
   literature.
Classification: LCC TT160 .K87425 2017 (print) | LCC TT160 (ebook) | DDC
   745.59--dc23
LC record available at http://lccn.loc.gov/2016000309

TO ADULT HELPERS

The craft projects in this series are fun and simple. There are just a few things to remember to keep kids safe. Some projects require the use of sharp or hot objects. Also, kids may be using messy materials such as glue or paint. Make sure they protect their clothes and work surfaces. Review the projects before starting, and be ready to assist when necessary.

KEY SYMBOL

Watch for this warning symbol in this book. Here is what it means.

HOT!

You will be working with something hot. Get help from an adult!

Super SandCastle™ books are created by a team of professional educators, reading specialists, and content developers around five essential components—phonemic awareness, phonics, vocabulary, text comprehension, and fluency—to assist young readers as they develop reading skills and strategies and increase their general knowledge. All books are written, reviewed, and leveled for guided reading and early reading intervention programs for use in shared, guided, and independent reading and writing activities to support a balanced approach to literacy instruction.

CONTENTS

Farm Critters   4

Get to Know Farm Animals!   6

Farm Animal Timeline   8

Materials   10

Smiley Happy Cow   12

Soft Fuzzy Sheep   14

Wild & Wacky Chicken   16

Pig Head Hat   20

Wise Springy Goat   22

Clip-Clop Horse   24

Classic Tubby Turkey   28

Flippy Flapping Goose   30

Glossary   32

FARM CRITTERS

Farm animals are cute and **cuddly**! They are soft to pet and fun to feed. They are useful too. Cows give us milk. Chickens give us eggs. Sheep give us wool and shorten the grass by eating it.

Wouldn't it be fun to have mini versions of your favorite farm animals? Make these easy crafts and create your own farm!

GET TO KNOW FARM ANIMALS!

FUN FACTS ABOUT COMMON FARM ANIMALS

SHEEP

Sheep have excellent vision. Their special pupils let them see nearly 360 **degrees**!

COWS

Cows are social animals. Like us, they form friendships within their herds.

PIGS

Pigs don't sweat. That's why they roll in the mud. Mud keeps them cool and protects them from sunburn.

GEESE

A baby goose is called a gosling. A group of geese is called a gaggle.

TURKEYS

Only male turkeys make a "gobble" sound. They use it to **attract** females.

GOATS

Goats are smart and curious. They often figure out how to escape their pens.

HORSES

Horses have long lives. Most live between 25 and 30 years.

CHICKENS

There are 25 **billion** chickens in the world. That is more than any other kind of bird.

FARM ANIMAL TIMELINE

WHERE AND WHEN FARM ANIMALS WERE FIRST RAISED

SHEEP

WHEN
11,000 years ago

WHERE
western Asia

ANCESTOR
Asiatic mouflon sheep

GOAT

WHEN
10,000 years ago

WHERE
western Asia

ANCESTOR
wild goat

PIG

WHEN
9,000 years ago

WHERE
Turkey, western Asia

ANCESTOR
wild boar

TURKEY

WHEN
3,000 years ago

WHERE
central Mexico

ANCESTOR
wild turkey

GOOSE

WHEN
4,000 years ago

WHERE
Europe,
northern Africa, Asia

ANCESTOR
greylag goose or
swan goose

HORSE

WHEN
6,000 years ago

WHERE
Russia, Kazakhstan,
Mongolia

ANCESTOR
wild horse

CATTLE

WHEN
8,000 years ago

WHERE
western Asia, India,
northern Africa

ANCESTOR
aurochs

CHICKEN

WHEN
8,000 years ago

WHERE
Southeast Asia,
China, India

ANCESTOR
red junglefowl

9

MATERIALS

HERE ARE SOME OF THE THINGS YOU'LL NEED TO DO THE PROJECTS.

acrylic paint

black marker

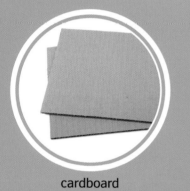
cardboard

chenille stems

clear tape

colored paper

craft glue

craft sticks

elastic

felt

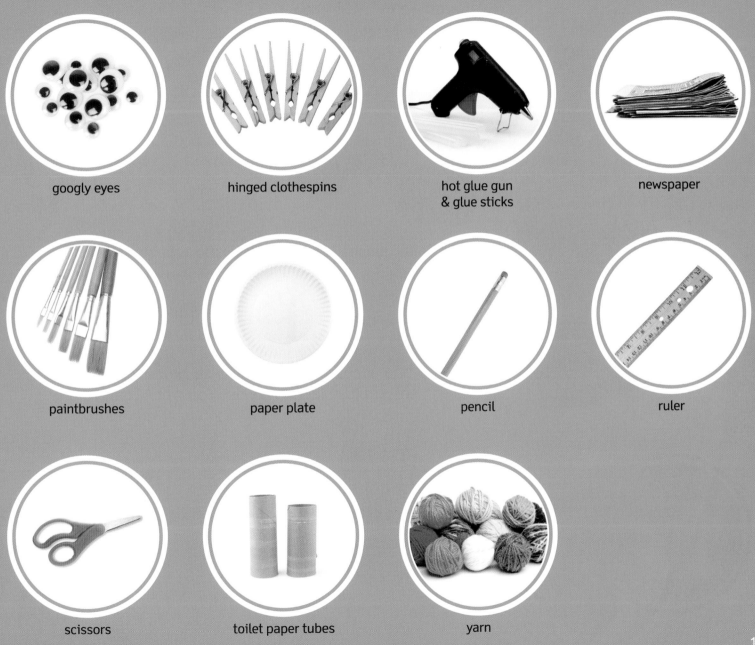

googly eyes

hinged clothespins

hot glue gun
& glue sticks

newspaper

paintbrushes

paper plate

pencil

ruler

scissors

toilet paper tubes

yarn

SMILEY HAPPY COW

THIS PAPER-PLATE COW WILL
make you smile every day!

MATERIALS

2 white paper plates   pink paper   black marker

scissors   craft glue   black paper

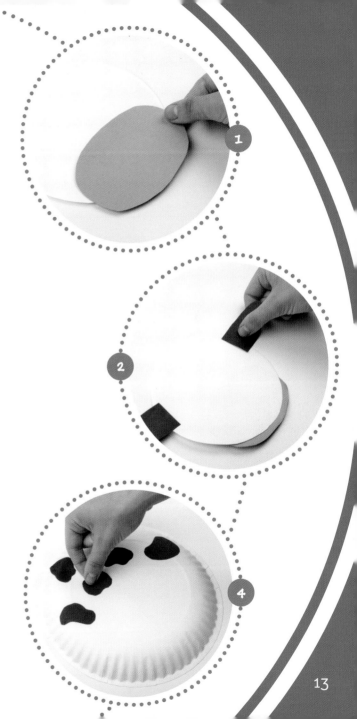

1. Cut the bottom out of one paper plate. Cut an oval out of pink paper. Make the oval about half the size of the white circle. Glue the pink oval to the bottom of the white circle. This is the cow's face.

2. Cut two rounded triangles out of black paper. Cut smaller rounded triangles out of pink paper. Glue a pink triangle to each black triangle. These are the ears. Glue them pink-side down to the back of the face. The ears should stick out on each side.

3. Draw **nostrils**, a mouth, and eyes on the face with a black marker.

4. Cut lumpy shapes that look like cow spots out of black paper. Turn the second paper plate upside down. Glue the spots to one half of the plate.

5. Glue the face to the blank half of the second paper plate. Let the glue dry.

SOFT FUZZY SHEEP

CUDDLE UP WITH THIS
WOOLLY FRIEND!

MATERIALS 🔥

white yarn	cardboard	black & brown felt
ruler	black chenille stem	2 googly eyes
scissors	hot glue gun & glue sticks	

1. Cut a piece of yarn 8 inches (20 cm) long. Cut a strip of cardboard. Make it 3 by 1½ inches (8 by 4 cm). Wrap yarn from the ball around the strip the short way 100 times. Cut the end of the yarn.

2. Slide the yarn off the cardboard, keeping it **bundled**. Tie the 8-inch (20 cm) piece of yarn tightly around the bundle.

3. Cut through the **loops** on each side. **Fluff** the yarn into a pom-pom. Trim any yarn that sticks out too far. This is the sheep's body.

4. Cut four pieces of chenille stem. Make each piece ¾ inch (2 cm) long. These are the legs. Glue them to the bottom of the body.

5. Cut an oval out of black felt. Make it 1 inch (3 cm) long. Cut off one end of the oval. Cut two small teardrop shapes out of black felt for the ears. Glue them to the round end of the oval.

6. Glue googly eyes to the face. Cut small circles out of brown felt for **nostrils**. Glue them to the face. Glue the face to the front of the sheep.

THIS LITTLE CHICK IS THE PERFECT PINT-SIZED PET!

MATERIALS 🔥

yellow yarn

ruler

scissors

cardboard

1 orange chenille stem

black & orange felt

hot glue gun
& glue sticks

1   Cut a piece of yarn 6 inches (15 cm) long. Cut a strip of cardboard. Make it 3 by 1½ inches (8 by 4 cm).

2   Wrap yarn from the ball around the strip the short way 75 times. Cut the end of the yarn.

3   Slide the yarn off the cardboard, keeping it **bundled**. Tie the 6-inch (15 cm) piece of yarn tightly around the bundle.

4   Cut through the **loops** on each side. **Fluff** the yarn into a pom-pom. Trim any yarn that sticks out too far. This is the chick's head.

(continued on next page)

5. Cut a piece of yarn 8 inches (20 cm) long. Wrap more yarn from the ball around the cardboard strip the short way 100 times. Cut the end of the yarn.

6. Repeat steps 3 and 4 to create another pom-pom. This is the chick's body.

7. Bend the chenille stem in half. Stick the ends through the center of the chick's head. Slide the head up until the folded end is hidden in the yarn.

8   Stick the ends of the stem through the body. Slide the body up to the head.

9   Bend the ends of the chenille stem to make the feet.

10   Cut two small circles out of black felt for eyes. Glue them onto the head.

11   Cut a small triangle out of orange felt for the beak. Glue it under the eyes. Let the glue dry.

PIG HEAD HAT

WEAR AN ADORABLE PIGGY
ON YOUR HEAD!

MATERIALS

pink paper

clear tape

scissors

dark pink, light
  pink & black
  felt

craft glue

ruler

black marker

pencil

1 pink chenille
  stem

elastic

1 Wrap the pink paper into a cone. Tape the edge in place. Cut the bottom of the cone to make it flat.

2 Cut two triangles out of dark pink felt. Cut two smaller triangles out of light pink felt. Glue them onto the large triangles. Glue the bottoms of the triangles to each side of the cone for ears.

3 Cut a strip of pink paper. Make it 4 by ½ inches (10 by 1 cm). Bend the strip into a circle. Tape the ends together. Cut a circle out of dark pink felt. Make it about the same size as the paper circle. Glue the edge of the paper circle to the felt circle. Glue the other edge onto the cone. This is the nose.

4 Cut two small circles out of black felt. Glue them to the nose. Draw two circles above the nose for eyes.

5 Wrap the chenille stem around the pencil. Remove the pencil. Use it to poke a hole in the back of the cone. Stick one end of the stem through the hole. Bend it inside the cone so it won't come out.

6 Poke a hole on each side of the cone. Cut a 12-inch (30 cm) piece of elastic. Tie one end through each hole.

21

WISE SPRINGY GOAT

PUT a SPRING In YOUR STEP BY
MAKING THIS TABLETOP GOAT!

MATERIALS

toilet paper tube	scissors	hot glue gun & glue sticks
gray acrylic paint	pencil	2 white chenille stems
paintbrush	1 gray chenille stem	black marker
ruler		

1. Paint the tube gray. Let it dry. Cut off a 3-inch (8 cm) piece of the tube.

2. Cut a 2-inch (5 cm) square out of the remaining part of the tube. Draw a head shape with ears on the cardboard square. Cut it out. Draw eyes, eyebrows, and a nose with black marker.

3. Cut two 1-inch (3 cm) pieces of gray chenille stem. Glue them to the back of the head between the ears. They are the horns.

4. Cut three ¾-inch (2 cm) pieces of white chenille stem. Glue them behind the goat's chin. These are the goat's beard.

5. Cut the second white chenille stem into four equal pieces. Wrap them around the pencil to make **coils**. Leave a little bit of one end of each piece straight. Glue the straight ends inside one end of the tube. Space them evenly.

6. Glue the head to the other end of the tube.

CLIP-CLOP HORSE

THIS CRAFTY HORSE WILL GALLOP INTO YOUR HEART!

MATERIALS 🔥

cardboard	black marker	paintbrush	1 hinged clothespin
ruler	newspaper	white yarn	
scissors	brown acrylic paint	hot glue gun & glue sticks	2 googly eyes
			4 craft sticks

1 Cut two 5-inch (13 cm) squares out of cardboard. Draw a horse's body on one square. Cut it out. Trace the shape on the other square. Cut it out.

2 Cover your work surface with newspaper. Lay one shape down with the head facing right. Paint the shape brown. Lay the other shape down with the head facing left. Paint the shape brown. Let the paint dry.

3 Cut 12 pieces of yarn for the mane. Make them 1½ inches (4 cm) long. Cut eight 3-inch (8 cm) pieces for the tail.

4 Lay one of the horse shapes painted-side down. Put glue along the head and neck. Stick one end of each mane yarn in the glue.

(continued on next page)

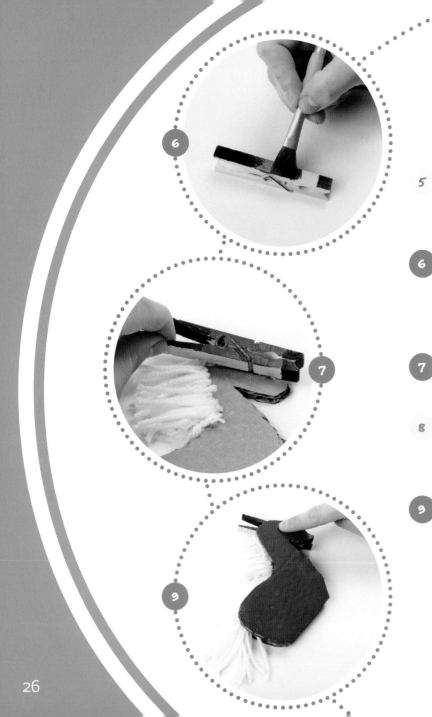

5   Put a **glob** of glue on the horse's behind. Stick one end of each tail yarn in the glue. Let the glue dry.

6   Color the handles of the clothespin with black marker. Color the tip of the **clamp** too. Paint the rest of the clothespin brown. Let the paint dry.

7   Glue the side of the clothespin to the horse's head.

8   Put glue all over the horse's body. Make sure to cover the other side of the clothespin and the yarn.

9   Press the other half of the body onto the glue. Let it dry.

10 Glue a googly eye on each side of the head.

11 Color one end of each craft stick black for the hooves.

12 Glue the other end of each stick to the horse for legs. Let the glue dry.

CLASSIC TUBBY TURKEY

MAKE A ROLY-POLY TURKEY!

MATERIALS

newspaper	paintbrush	ruler
1 paper plate	scissors	craft glue
brown acrylic paint	colored paper	2 googly eyes

1 Cover your work surface with newspaper. Paint the bottom of the paper plate brown. Let the paint dry. Cut out the center of the plate.

2 Cut feather shapes out of colored paper. Make each one 5 inches (13 cm) long. Glue one end of each feather to the back of the plate. Go about halfway around the plate. **Alternate** colors.

3 Cut two turkey feet out of orange paper. Glue them to the back of the plate. Make sure they stick off the bottom edge.

4 Cut a small triangle out of orange paper for the beak. Cut a small oval out of pink paper for the **wattle**.

5 Turn the turkey face up. Glue the beak and wattle to the middle of the turkey. The beak should **overlap** the wattle slightly. Glue the googly eyes above the beak. Let the glue dry.

make a gaggle to make
you giggle!

MATERIALS

3 white paper plates   ruler   orange paper

scissors   pencil   black marker

craft glue

1. Cut one paper plate in half. These are the wings. Glue one end of each wing to the back of the second paper plate. Make sure the flat sides face the same direction.

2. Lay the third plate face down. Make two marks on the edge 4½ inches (11 cm) apart. Draw a line from each mark toward the center of the plate, stopping before they touch. This is the goose's neck. Draw a circle above the ends of the lines. Cut out the entire shape. This is the goose's neck and head.

3. Glue the edge of the neck to the back of the paper plate above the of the wings.

4. Cut a triangle out of orange paper for the beak. Glue it to the goose's head. Draw eyes with black marker.

5. Cut feet out of orange paper. Glue them behind the bottom of the body.

31

GLOSSARY

alternate – to change back and forth from one to the other.

attract – to cause someone or something to come near.

billion – a very large number. One billion is also written 1,000,000,000.

bundle – a group of things tied together.

clamp – something that holds or presses things together.

coil – a spiral or a series of loops.

cuddly – good to hold close because of being soft or warm.

degree – a unit used to measure how far something turns. One complete turn is 360 degrees.

fluff – to loosen or separate strands of hair or yarn.

glob – a large drop of something.

loop – a circle made by something such as yarn, string, or wire.

nostril – an opening in the nose.

overlap – to lie partly on top of something.

wattle – the flap of skin that hangs from the neck of some birds.